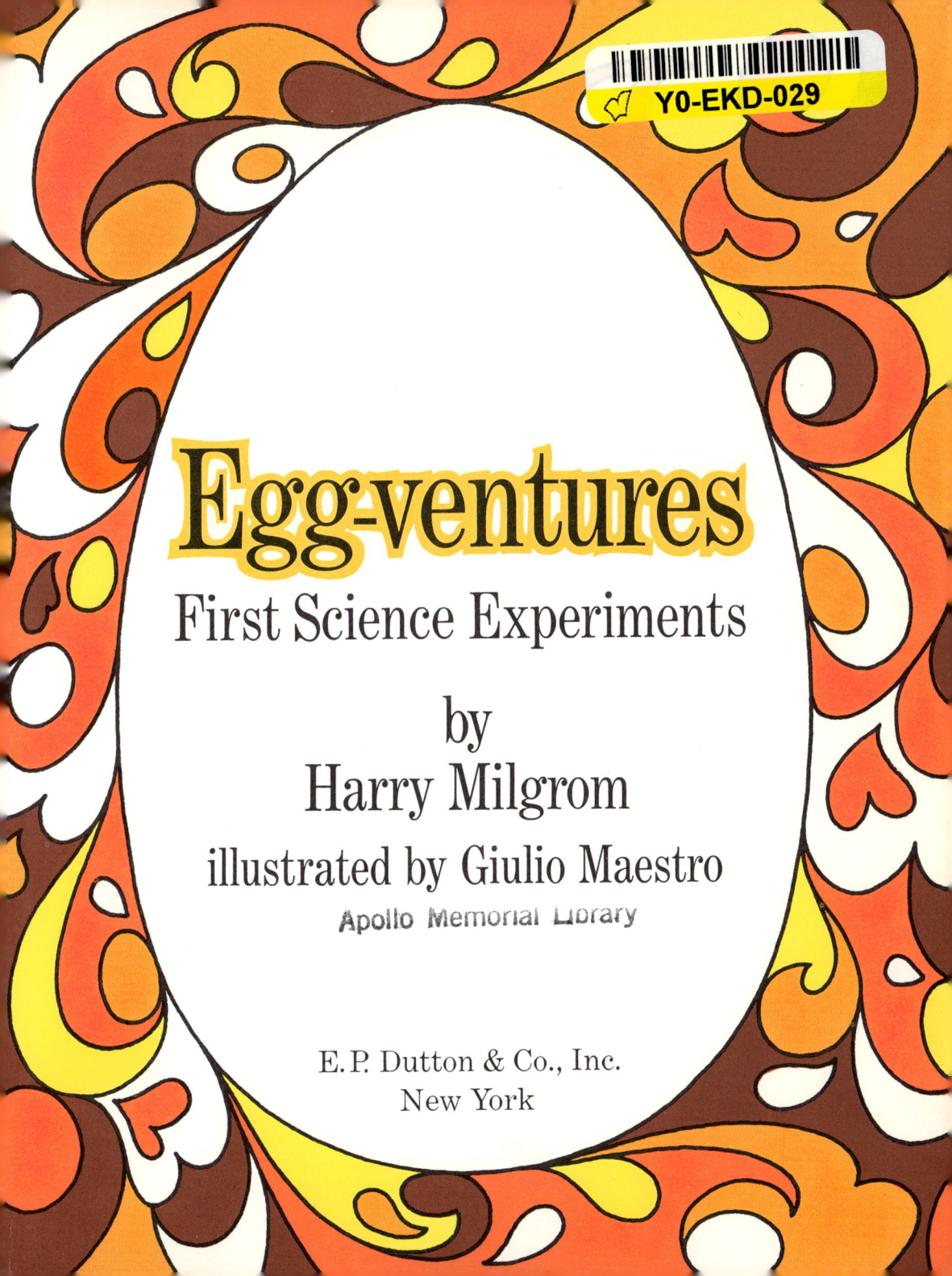

Egg-ventures

First Science Experiments

by
Harry Milgrom

illustrated by Giulio Maestro

E. P. Dutton & Co., Inc.
New York

*To my dear wife Betty
and our newest grandson,
Daniel Joshua*

Text copyright © 1974 by Harry Milgrom
Illustrations copyright © 1974 by Giulio Maestro

All rights reserved. No part of this publication may be reproduced or transmitted in any form or by any means, electronic or mechanical, including photocopy, recording, or any information storage and retrieval system now known or to be invented, without permission in writing from the publisher, except by a reviewer who wishes to quote brief passages in connection with a review written for inclusion in a magazine, newspaper, or broadcast.

Library of Congress Cataloging in Publication Data

Milgrom, Harry   Egg-ventures.

SUMMARY: Instructions for simple experiments that reveal the characteristics of an egg.

1. Eggs—Experiments—Juvenile literature   [1. Eggs—Experiments]   I. Maestro, Giulio, illus.   II. Title.
SF490.M54   641.3'7'54   74-5231   ISBN 0-525-29160-1

Published simultaneously in Canada by Clarke, Irwin & Company Limited, Toronto and Vancouver

Designed by Giulio Maestro
Printed in the U.S.A.   First Edition

10   9   8   7   6   5   4   3   2   1

An egg is good for eating.
It is also good for exploring.

Be an egg explorer.
Do the experiments in this book.

Ask your mother, father, or other grown-up to hard-boil several eggs for you. You will also need a number of raw eggs. Use the hard-boiled eggs, unless the experiment calls for a raw egg. Set up your laboratory on a table. Cover the table to protect it.

Hold a hard-boiled chicken egg in your hand.
What is the color of the egg?
It may be white or brown.
How does it feel?

The egg feels smooth and curved. It has no edges or corners.

How long is the egg?
Put the egg lengthways between the backs of two books. With a ruler measure the distance between the books. That's the length of the egg.

How wide is the egg?
Put the egg sideways between the books. With the ruler measure the distance between the books again. This time the distance is the same as the width of the egg.

What is the shape of the egg?
Place the egg on its side on a sheet of paper.
With a pencil draw a line around the egg.

The line forms a figure that is called egg-shaped or oval.

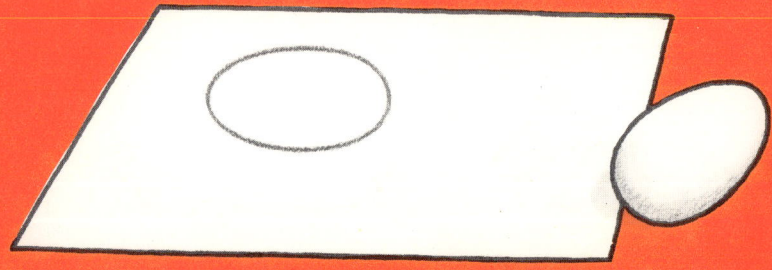

How much space does your egg take up?
Pour 1½ cups of water into a 2-cup measuring cup. Place your egg in the water.
What happens to the level of the water?
The water rises from the 1½-cup mark to the 1¾-cup mark.

Here is what happens. The egg and the water cannot be in the same space at the same time. So the egg pushes up an amount of water equal to the space the egg takes up. In this example the egg pushes up ¼ cup of water.
This means the egg takes up ¼ cup of space.

Does your raw egg sink or float in water?
Use the same measuring cup with 1½ cups of
water in it. Place your egg in the water.
What does the egg do?

It sinks to the bottom if the egg is fresh.
If the egg is very rotten, it floats in the water.
This is one way to tell a fresh egg from a rotten
one without cracking open the eggs.

How can you make a fresh raw egg float in water?
Add table salt to the water in the measuring cup.
Dissolve 1 level teaspoonful of salt at a time.
After each spoonful see what the egg does in the
water. When you have dissolved about 10 teaspoonsful of salt the egg will float in the water.
A fresh egg floats in salt water. People also float
more easily in the salt water of an ocean than
in the unsalted water of a lake.

In which position does a hard-boiled egg rest without rolling?
Place the egg on one end.
What does the egg do? It rolls.
Place the egg on the other end.
What happens? The egg rolls.

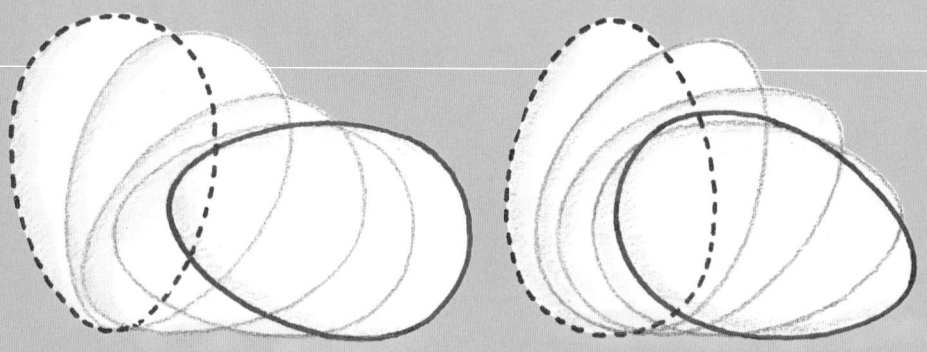

Place the egg on its side.
What does the egg do now? On its side the egg rests without rolling.

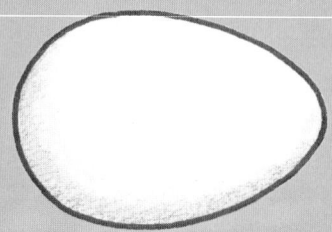

How can you make an egg stand on its end?
Heap a little pile of salt on the table.
Press the end of a hard-boiled egg into the mound. Let go of the egg.
What happens? The egg remains standing because the salt supports it.

How does an egg roll?
Set a hard-boiled egg on the table.
Give the egg a gentle push.
What does the egg do? As the egg rolls, it wobbles from side to side. It does not move in a straight line.

Now set a ball on the table.
Give the ball a gentle push.
What does the ball do? The ball does not wobble. It rolls in a straight line.

An oval object (egg) cannot be rolled as easily as a round object (ball). That is why eggs, not balls, are used in egg-rolling contests.

Where do chicken eggs come from?
Chicken eggs are made and laid by mother chickens called hens.

What are chicken eggs?
Some eggs contain unborn chicks. Such eggs give the chicks food and protection before they hatch.

It takes about 21 days for a baby chick to hatch
from an egg. During this incubation period
the egg must be turned and kept warm and moist.
The mother hen does this naturally when
she sits on the egg.

Eggs can also be cared for and hatched in a
special container known as an incubator.

Some eggs do not contain unborn chicks.
They are used as food for people.

What is inside a food egg?
Ask a grown-up to help you open a raw egg.
Empty the egg into a dish. What do you see?

You see a clear liquid around a yellow blob.
Save the raw egg for the next experiment.

What does heat do to the liquid parts of an egg?
With the help of a grown-up fry the liquid insides
of the egg in a pan. Try not to break the yellow part.
What happens as the pan gets hot?
The clear liquid changes quickly into a white solid.
That is why the clear liquid is known as the white
of the egg.

Next, cover the pan. After about five minutes lift the cover and look at the egg. What do you see? The yellow part has also changed from a liquid to a solid.
Have the fried egg for lunch.

What does beating do to the clear liquid of an egg? Ask your adult helper to separate the clear liquid from the yellow blob. Whip the liquid with an egg-beater.

What change do you notice?
The colorless liquid becomes a thick, white foam. What does this? The egg-beater forces air into the sticky liquid. Thousands of air bubbles are trapped in the liquid. The bubbles and the tiny drops of liquid cling together to make the foam.

What are the parts of a food egg?
There is a hard shell on the outside of the egg.
Look at the shell through a magnifying glass.
What do you see?
The shell is not smooth. It has many small bumps and dents. It also has invisible holes that let air move in and out.

Next, peel the shell off a hard-boiled egg.
Cut the egg in half along its length.
What do you find inside?

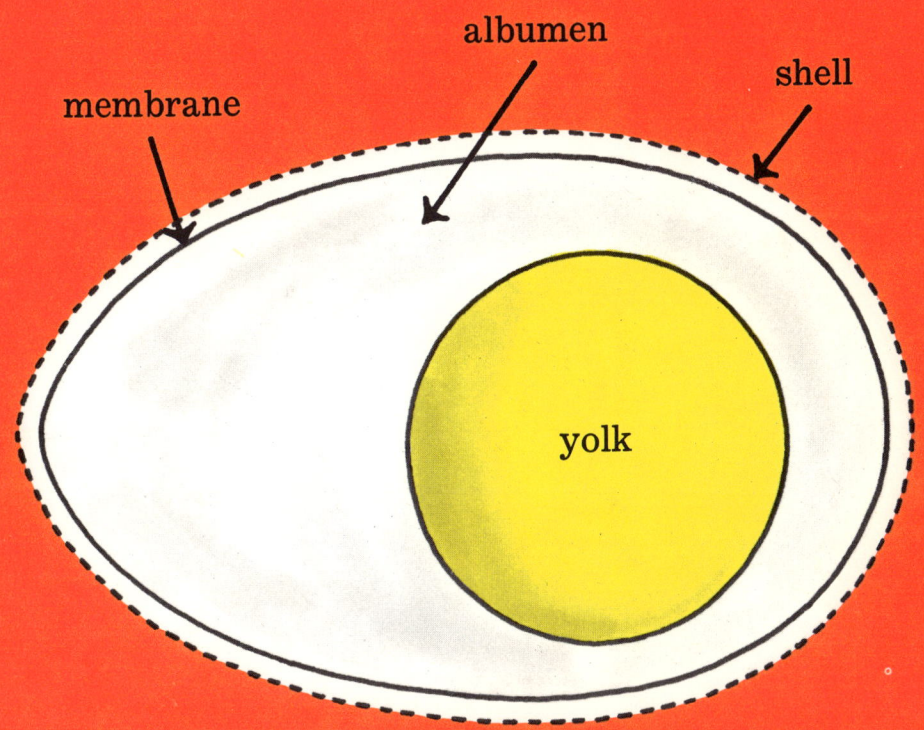

Right under the shell there is a thin, rubbery skin. It is the egg membrane. Then comes the white of the egg. It is the albumen.
The last part is the yellow center. It is the egg yolk.
So you see the food egg has four main parts.

Why do we eat food eggs? We need nutrients, vitamins, and minerals in the food we eat. From the albumen and yolk of an egg we get these materials:

    nutrients — protein and fat
    vitamins — A, B1, B2, and D
    minerals — copper, iron, and phosphorus

How are eggs graded?
Eggs are graded by quality.
    Grade AA — excellent
    Grade A — good
    Grade B — watery
    Grade C — more watery

Eggs are also graded by weight.
A jumbo egg weighs about 2½ ounces.
An extra large egg weighs about 2¼ ounces.
A large egg weighs about 2 ounces.
A medium egg weighs about 1¾ ounces.
A small egg weighs about 1½ ounces.
A peewee egg weighs about 1¼ ounces.

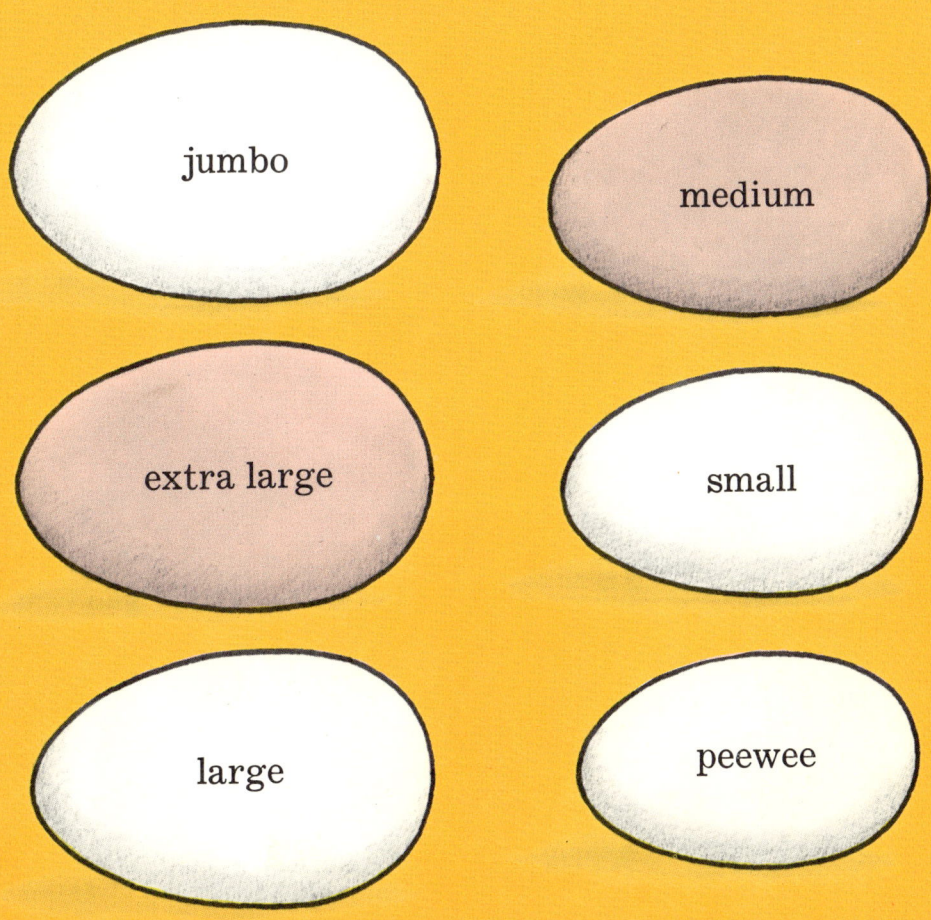

How can you tell the difference between a hard-boiled egg and a raw egg?
On the table place a raw egg next to a hard-boiled egg. Look at the two eggs. Can you see which is which by looking?

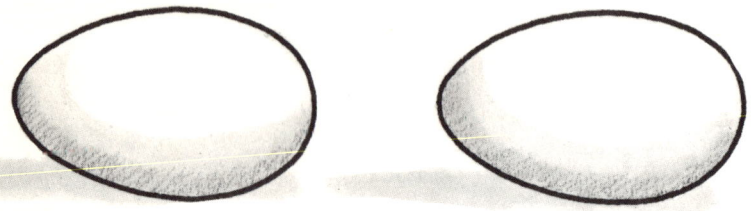

They look the same.
Shake each egg. Can you feel which is which?
You may feel or hear the liquid move in the raw egg. It is not easy to tell the difference
by shaking.

In a darkened room hold each egg close to
the beam of a flashlight.
What do you notice?

More light shines through the raw egg than
through the hard-boiled egg. This method of looking
into eggs is called candling because candlelight
was used at one time.

Spin each egg.
What happens?

The hard-boiled egg spins faster and longer than the raw egg. The loose liquid in the raw egg acts like a brake.
The spin test is an easy way to tell the difference between the two eggs.

How can you decorate an egg?
Take a hard-boiled egg. Draw on the shell.
Try using these things.

pencil

pen

crayon

chalk

brush with food colors

Use the ones you like best to decorate
your own eggs.

Now you know what a marvelous thing an egg is.
A chicken egg is made and laid by a hen.

A chicken egg has an oval shape.
A raw egg sinks in unsalted water.
An egg cannot stand on its end by itself.
An egg can stand on its end in a small pile of salt.

An egg wobbles when it rolls.
Some eggs contain unborn chicks.
Some eggs are used as food for people.

The liquids in an egg become solid when the egg is heated.

An egg has four main parts.
Food eggs are graded by quality and weight.
A food egg contains nutrients, vitamins, and minerals.
A raw egg lets light pass through.
A hard-boiled egg spins better than a raw egg.
An egg shell can be decorated.

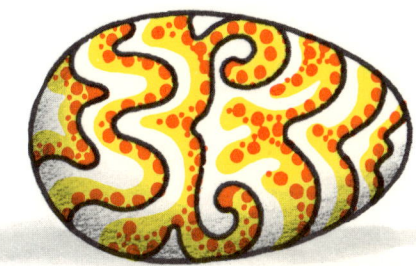

What else can you find out about an egg?
Think of what you want to know.
Do an experiment.
See what amazing things you can discover.

HARRY MILGROM is Director of Science for the New York City public schools. He has devised many new materials and techniques for teaching science and is also founding director of Science I, a Saturday program for children that he conducts at the Dalton School in Manhattan. His *Adventures with* series includes first science experiments with many objects: a ball, a cardboard tube, a paper cup, a party plate, a plastic bag, a straw, and a string.

GIULIO MAESTRO has been illustrating fulltime since 1969, when he left the advertising design field. Among the picture books he has written and illustrated are *The Tortoise's Tug of War* and *The Remarkable Plant in Apartment 4*. He has also illustrated many other books for children—from craft and science books to folktales. He and his wife live in Madison, Connecticut.

The display type is set in Century Nova and the text type in Ideal. The art is three-color preseparated, and the book was printed by offset at Pearl Pressman Liberty.